Life With God

BEING THE CHURCH

David L. Zercher

Evangel Press
2000 Evangel Way
Nappanee, Indiana 46550-0189

Cover photograph: Mooretown (Mich.) Brethren in Christ Church

Cover design: Glen Pierce

Library of Congress Catalog Card Number: 90-082382

ISBN: 0-916035-40-9

PHOTOTYPESET FOR QUALITY

Printed in the United States of America

5 4 3 2 1

Contents

Introduction

Perhaps the reason you are reading this book is that you are thinking about joining the church. You have committed your life to Jesus and feel good about the church you're attending. What better way to affirm the former and express the latter than to join the church?

While joining is a good and appropriate way to affirm your commitment to God and your fellow believers, the best way to do that is not to *join* the church, it's to *be* the church.

These are, in fact, two very different concepts. Many of us know people who have joined the church for the wrong reasons. What's more, some people join the church on paper but not in practice. But *being* the church means you are part of the adventure.

This book will describe that adventure and challenge you to be a part of it. I hope this study will encourage you to join your local church roster. But the focus is on living out that commitment in accordance with the Brethren in Christ understanding of *being* a responsible member of the body of Christ. Sometimes this will seem to be a rather rigorous adventure. Indeed, like any adventure, it will require effort. But as you utilize this material, you will glimpse not only the rigors but also the joys of being a responsible member of a local Brethren in Christ church.

This study, *Being the Church*, is the third book in the *Life With God* series. While it is not assumed you have read the first two books in the series (*Basics for New Christians* and *Love in Action*), the ideas and principles they contain should not be foreign to you. Therefore, you may find it beneficial to have them nearby for an occasional review and/or cross-reference.

David Zercher

The Membership Covenant

The Brethren in Christ Church has, as most churches do, a statement which all its members affirm. This covenant represents the most important aspects of being a member of the Brethren in Christ Church. It should therefore be considered with care by each person exploring membership:

> *As a member of the Brethren in Christ Church, I accept the Bible as the Word of God in which is revealed the way of salvation and the guide for faith and conduct. I witness to a personal experience of God's saving grace in my heart and express desire and purpose to live a holy life, apart from sin and separated unto Christ. I covenant as a member of the Brethren in Christ Church to be loyal to this congregation, to consent to instruction in Bible doctrine, to support and sustain the services of the congregation by my regular attendance and prayers, to contribute to her program as the Lord prospers me, and to foster a spirit of Christian fellowship and oneness within the Church.*

Our study is based upon the covenant above. It won't always follow the written order of the covenant, but it will deal with the covenant in its entirety. The covenant vows lie in two specific areas: first, in the kind of people we ought to be (Chapters 1-3); and, second, in the kinds of things we ought to do to build a healthy Christian community (Chapters 4-5).

Each chapter (except for Chapter 6) begins with a particular statement drawn from the covenant; each chapter ends with questions for reflection as well as an opportunity to affirm that portion of the covenant statement. Prayerfully consider the commitment you're asked to make before you sign your name.

1

Be Reconciled to God

"As a member of the Brethren in Christ Church, . . . I witness to a personal experience of God's saving grace in my heart.

Of all the joys we experience in this life, those arising from family and friendships are some of the very best. Loving, stable relationships bring security, peace, and assurance. They bless us with abundant life more than possessions or success ever can.

Of all the sufferings we endure as human beings, few are as severe as the pain of broken relationships. Whether it be with a parent or a child, a spouse or a friend, the simple fact of the matter is this: broken relationships hurt.

Perhaps you've experienced that pain. Perhaps you have even experienced the heartache of being repeatedly rebuffed in your attempts to bring healing to a relationship gone sour. If that is the case, then you've tasted a bit of what God experiences regularly, for God continually seeks reconciliation with sinful people who have turned their backs and walked away.

A prodigal son and a gracious father

Who is God? And what is God like? It's impossible to describe God with one little story, but Jesus' parable of the prodigal son (Luke 15:11-32) provides us with some valuable insights. In this familiar story, Jesus speaks of a son who, for reasons of pride and selfishness, left his home and father. After a long period of time, the son returns, setting the stage for his father's response: while the prodigal son "was still a long way off, his father saw him and was filled with compassion for him; he ran to his son, threw his arms around him and kissed him" (Luke 15:20).

Who then is God? The parable of the prodigal son tells us that God is One who lovingly receives his wayward children into his arms, One who is always ready and willing for reconciliation to take place, and One who rejoices when it does.

The gospel is good news!

Perhaps you know the parable of the prodigal son well enough to remember there is another character in the story: the prodigal's older brother. The older brother usually is viewed as a nasty person, but it would be more accurate to see him as a person who simply wants justice. It goes against his (and our) sense of justice to see this wayward son welcomed—even rewarded—after squandering his family's wealth.

But that is what grace is all about. The gospel of Jesus Christ is a gospel of grace, boldly proclaiming: "What you get is not what you deserve." In fact, to be a Christian means coming to the realization that God gives humanity an incredibly generous offer. A large portion of the Bible is devoted to describing that offer:

—We are sinners (Romans 3:23), separated from God (Isaiah 59:2). We deserve death (Romans 6:23a).

—"While we were still sinners, Christ died for us" (Romans 5:8).

—Through Christ's death, we can be reconciled to God and therefore "be saved through his life!" (Romans 5:10).

To receive reconcilation with God, however, we must first acknowledge our rebellion (1 John 1:9) and submit to the Lordship of Jesus Christ (Romans 10:9). The Apostle Paul calls for this in 2 Corinthians 5: "Be reconciled to God." Why? Because "God was reconciling the world to himself in Christ, not counting men's sins against them (2 Cor. 5:19). It is by God's grace alone that we who are *in Christ Jesus* are spared the punishment that we deserve.

Brothers and sisters "in Christ"

The Brethren in Christ believe this good news. In fact, that's what we mean when we say we're "Brethren *in Christ*." It's this "in-Christ-ness" that binds us together as brothers and sisters (see John 1:12-13). The church is a body of believers—a family—who trust in Jesus Christ as Savior and Lord. He's our common bond, and a wonderful bond he is!

Being brothers and sisters in Christ implies many ideas and actions that we'll touch on throughout this book. For one, it

Jesus' Death on the Cross Brought . . .

Image	*Setting*	*Definition*	*Reference*
Reconciliation	Relationship	"to bring together"	Romans 5:10
Justification	Courtroom	"to release from penalty"	Romans 5:1
Redemption	Marketplace	"to buy back"	Col. 1:13-14 Mark 10:45
Regeneration	Birthing room	"to be born again"	John 3:3-6 2 Cor. 5:17
Propitiation (or atoning sacrifice)	Temple altar	"to appease anger"	Romans 3:25 1 John 4:10

implies that we all have been converted. Conversion means a change of heart—the conscious rejection of a life of sin and a turning to the one who can forgive sin and give new life, Jesus Christ. This is called repentance.

For some Christians, repentance is a dramatic experience. God's graciousness and their own sinfulness confront them rather suddenly and they turn to God. For others, that experience is a process in which, over time, the Spirit leads them to trust in Jesus. Still others (e.g., some who were raised in Christian homes) cannot remember a time in their lives when they didn't believe in Jesus. Yet they rejoice in the privilege of being raised in communities of faith, communities which nurtured them in such a way that, at the proper time, they adopted that faith as their own.

Regardless of how one comes to faith, the Brethren in Christ firmly believe that each person is responsible before God as an individual. In other words, each person must ultimately make the decision to follow Jesus for him or herself. The faith of one's parents, friends and/or church may be instructive and encouraging, but personal faith is necessary.

An owned faith, a shared faith

True faith, therefore, must be an *owned* faith; it must be personally experienced and life changing. It must just as certainly be a *shared* faith, shared with those inside the church as well as those outside the church (see Chapter 6). Sharing within the church is done in many ways. Among them is the ordinance of baptism.

Whereas some Christian churches advocate the baptism of infants, the Brethren in Christ practice "believers' baptism"; that is, the baptism of those who have already received Jesus into their lives. Believers' baptism offers an outward sign of what God has already done in the heart of the believer and therefore serves as a testimony to those who have gathered to worship. Without a doubt, the service of baptism should be a time of rejoicing in the church as brothers and sisters in Christ celebrate the joy of new birth and reconciliation with God and one another.

Another way we illustrate the bond of sharing is by observing the Lord's Supper. The Lord's Supper is a simple meal patterned after the one Jesus shared with his disciples the night he was betrayed (Luke 22:14-23). Together, they ate bread, representing Christ's soon-to-be broken body; together, they drank wine, representing his soon-to-be shed blood. And because Jesus commanded his disciples to "do this in remembrance" of him, his present day disciples do the same—eat the bread, drink the cup, and recall his death, *together*. This is "communion"—celebrating our mutual gift of salvation, a gift that makes us brothers and sisters in Christ.

Conclusion

Just as a child must experience a physical birth to live, so too must we experience a spiritual birth to live; and just as a child cannot accomplish that on his or her own, so too are we incapable of giving ourselves the gift of life. But thanks to God's gracious gift, we are reconciled to him and can live joyously and eternally as God's children.

Questions for reflection:

1. The parable of the prodigal son (Luke 15:11-32) is one of Jesus' most familiar parables. In what ways does the response of the prodigal's father correspond with God's response to us? In what ways does the analogy fall short?

2. If you were asked to sum up the message of salvation in four or five concise sentences, how would you do it? Take a few minutes to think about it and then write it down.

3. The text states that conversion experiences of Christians are *not* all the same. Recall your conversion experience. Would you describe it as a crisis? a process? Or is there yet a better way to describe it?

4. Read Paul's account of the Lord's Supper in 1 Corinthians 11:17-34. What is the purpose of the Lord's Supper? How were the Corinthians celebrating it inappropriately? How might we celebrate it inappropriately?

A testimony to offer

I, ______________________________, witness to a personal experience of God's saving grace in my heart.

2

Be People of the Book

"As a member of the Brethren in Christ Church, I accept the Bible as the Word of God in which is revealed the way of salvation and the guide for faith and conduct."

Bible conferences, Bible camps, Bible studies, Bible quizzing, Bible School—five activities which have played or which currently play significant roles in the life of the Brethren in Christ Church. Their common denominator? The Bible, of course. The Bible—to some who read it, an utterly ordinary book, but to those who read it with eyes of faith, an extraordinary book indeed.

The Bible in Brethren in Christ history

From their very beginning, the Brethren in Christ have attested to the extraordinary nature of the Bible. Accounts of Brethren in Christ origins paint pictures of a small band of men and women huddled near the Susquehanna River in Pennsylvania, but, more importantly, huddled around the Word of God. There, gathered around the Word, they came face to face with

God and his grace, with themselves and their need. It was there, huddled around the Word, that they discovered who they were, who they should be and what they should be doing. Our ancestors were unquestionably "people of the Book."

Today, we continue to make that claim. Our doctrinal statement attests to the authority of God's divinely inspired Word and acknowledges that the Scriptures are the Christian's ultimate source of truth, purpose, and direction. These forthright statements indicate that, in the years ahead just as in the years gone by, the Brethren in Christ will be "people of the Book."

The Bible as our authority

Being people of the Book, however, is easier said than done. Living under any moral authority, let alone the moral authority of ancient writings, is not a welcome thought in our society. We look around and instead discover a world which has adopted as its operating principle the last verse in the book of Judges: "Everyone [does] what is right in his own eyes." And when you live in a world like that, it's easy to live that way yourself.

The problem—let's call it "moral anarchy"—is a serious problem. It's not a new one, however, for it was precisely that problem which compelled Paul to write his second letter to Timothy. At the outset of 2 Timothy 3, Paul warns his young brother in the Lord to beware of moral anarchists: people who are "lovers of themselves, lovers of money, boastful, proud, abusive . . . always learning but never able to acknowledge the truth" (2 Tim. 3:2-7). The situation should sound familiar to us today: society's moral fabric was rotting because people refused to "acknowledge the truth."

Paul's advice to Timothy was straightforward and simple: Timothy was to continue in the ways of the holy Scriptures, ways he had been taught since infancy. Thanks in part to his grandmother Lois and his mother Eunice, Timothy had become over the years a "person of the Book." Now that he was no longer a boy but a leader in the church, the Scriptures were to serve as his defense in the battle against moral anarchy.

The purpose of the Bible

The Scriptures are our defense against moral anarchy, too. As they had for Timothy, the Scriptures have for us a threefold purpose. First of all, the Scriptures have been given to make people "wise for salvation through faith in Jesus Christ" (2 Timothy 3:15). While it's possible to appreciate the literature of the Bible and be stimulated by its stories without a conversion experience, the person who reads solely for pleasure and/or intellectual stimulation neglects the Bible's fundamental reason for existence: to help people "see" Jesus and be saved.

There are countless examples of the Bible fulfilling this purpose, sometimes in rather surprising ways. Take, for example, the philosopher Emile Cailliet. As a soldier and veteran of World War I, Cailliet's all-consuming desire was to find a book that would "understand" him. When he couldn't find such a book, he undertook to write it himself, but found his own efforts to be as futile as the efforts of others.

Having given up hope of ever finding a book that would understand him, Cailliet despaired, but God intervened: Cailliet's wife brought home a Bible and she gave it to her husband. This is what Cailliet later wrote:

> *I opened it and "chanced" upon the Beatitudes! I read and read and read. . . . And suddenly the realization dawned upon me: This* was *the Book that would understand me! . . . I continued to read deeply into the night, mostly from the gospels. And lo and behold, as I looked through them, the One of whom they spoke, the One who spoke and acted in them, became alive to me.*[1]

The Bible had made Emile Cailliet "wise for salvation through faith in Jesus Christ."

The second purpose of the Bible is to serve as our spiritual "coach." Much like a softball coach helps her players become better hitters and fielders, the Bible helps its readers become stronger Christians by "teaching, rebuking, correcting and training in righteousness" (2 Timothy 3:16). Those four verbs (teaching, rebuking, correcting, and training) represent both sides of doctrinal and ethical instruction, the positive and the negative side:

	Positive	***Negative***
Doctrinal beliefs	*teaching* right ideas	*rebuking* wrong ideas
Ethical behavior	*training* for right actions	*correcting* wrong actions

Part of what makes a coach a good coach is her willingness to *affirm* her players' right moves and *correct* their wrong ones. Part of what makes the Bible a good book is its ability to do the same.

A third, and closely related, function of the Bible is its equipping function. In other words, teaching, rebuking, correcting and training should never be seen as ends in themselves but rather as means to equip God's people "for every good work" (2 Timothy 3:17). Bible study is indeed an inward discipline, a discipline that's done for the good of one's own soul. Yet Bible study also should have an effect on our neighbors. When we study the Bible seriously and take its message seriously, good works spread throughout the church and throughout the world.

The Church as the interpretive community

It is one thing to say (as the Brethren in Christ do) that the Bible is our guide for faith and conduct; it is another thing altogether to agree on the meaning of specific biblical passages and their application to our lives. Whether we like it or not, the need for interpretation is a fundamental component of written language; consequently, the interpretive task (*hermeneutical task* is another widely used term) is one of the primary responsibilities of the church.

Unlike some religious groups (Christian and non-Christian alike), the Brethren in Christ have given interpretive authority to the community itself. In other words, interpretive decisions are made not primarily by our scholars nor by our church hierarchy, but by brothers and sisters gathered around the Word, seeking the mind of Christ. We interpret the Bible *together*, not as "Lone

Rangers." Therefore, the Brethren in Christ Church strongly encourages its members to attend Sunday school and participate in group Bible study, environments in which the people of God can dig into the Word and collectively weigh its meanings.

The interpretive community—an important concept to the Brethren in Christ—might be summed up this way:

In his mercy, the Lord has given us his Word.
In his wisdom, the Lord has given us one another.
In his church, we carry out the interpretive task.

Conclusion

The interpretive task is a never-ending one. As our world changes, so do our understandings and applications of the Scriptures. Therefore, as much as we might like to, the Brethren in Christ will never "corner the market" on biblical truth and understanding. God's expectation, however, is not a "full understanding" of his Word; his expectation is that we "fully stand under" his Word, submitting ourselves to its doctrinal and ethical claims as we understand them.

As God, by his Spirit, enlightens us and increases our understanding, he expects us to do his will. People who are truly "people of the Book" will do no less.

Questions for reflection:

1. Do you agree with the assertion that in our society "everyone does what is right in his own eyes?" Why or why not?

2. Was there a "Lois," a "Eunice" or a "Paul" in your life—that is, someone who helped you become a "person of the Book"? Have you in turn helped someone else discover the truths of the Scriptures?

3. Reread the story of Emile Cailliet on page 14. What do you think Cailliet meant when he wrote that the Bible "was the Book that would understand me"? How does the Bible "understand" you?

4. What is your current involvement with the Scriptures? Do you have personal Bible study time built into your schedule? Do you have Bible study time with other believers built into your schedule?

An acknowledgement to make

I, ______________________________, accept the Bible as the Word of God in which is revealed the way of salvation and the guide for faith and conduct.

---

[1]Emile Cailliet, *Journey Into Light* (Grand Rapids, MI: Zondervan, 1968), p. 18.

3

Be Holy

"As a member of the Brethren in Christ Church, I . . . express desire and purpose to live a holy life, apart from sin and separated unto Christ."

"I covenant as a member of the Brethren in Christ Church to . . . consent to instruction in Bible doctrine. . . ."

One of the most commonly-asked questions in Western society is: What do you want to be when you grow up? Just about the time young people begin to comprehend the fact that there are such things as occupations, their well-intentioned parents, grandparents, aunts and uncles begin to pester them with that all-important and ever-nagging question. It's a question which frequently lingers in the mind long after one's body has grown up.

God doesn't necessarily want to pester us, but being the parent that he is, he too is concerned with what we're going to be when we grow up. Unlike many earthly parents, though, his concern rests not so much with our earthly occupations (what we're going to *do*) as with our spiritual calling (what we're called to *be*). In fact, that's his number one concern: our spiritual well-*being*. It's a concern which can be ignored and even rejected, but if God gets his way with us, we'll be holy.[1]

Being holy

Holiness is a biblical word representing (1) who God is and (2) what he desires his people to be. This dual meaning of holiness can be seen in God's word to the people of Israel in Leviticus 20:26: "*You are to be holy* to me because *I, the Lord, am holy* and I have set you apart from the nations to be my own."

That verse (Leviticus 20:26) offers one of the best and most concise definitions of the word "holy": it means to be "set apart." God, in his purity, is "set apart from sinners" (Hebrews 7:26), entirely unique in his blamelessness. But God doesn't rest contentedly in his own holiness; he goes further than that, setting apart from sin those who place their trust in him. In the Old Testament, we see God's mercy rather specifically extended to the nation of Israel, which was for him "a holy nation" (Exodus 19:6). In the New Testament, this mercy is extended through Jesus Christ to the ends of the earth, for it is God's desire that "we may share in his holiness" (Hebrews 12:10). Holiness, then, is a gift of God through Jesus Christ our Lord. It is God who provides the resources for us to live holy lives, and it is by his power that we are set apart from sin.

Consecration and discipleship

Nonetheless, we shouldn't begin to think that God does everything while we do nothing. *Consecration* is our part. Consecration, as one Brethren in Christ writer has aptly written, is "the hallowing of God's name in all of life. It means that the choices of life are made from the perspective of God's kingdom. It makes 'Thy will be done' the highest priority in one's life."[2]

The words "Thy will be done" are prominent in the life of Christ. Not only did Jesus teach his disciples to pray that way (Matthew 6:10), he himself prayed that way at his life's most crucial juncture (Matthew 26:36-46). "Thy will be done" was, to Jesus, much more than just a Sunday morning prayer.

And so it must be to us. If we are to be holy, we, like Jesus, must pray that prayer in everyday matters, as well as at life's most crucial turns. That's not always an easy thing to do, but God has promised that as we follow Christ's example in prayer, the Holy Spirit will equip us to follow Christ's example in life. That, in sum, is what it means to be a disciple: following Jesus' example in all of life.

It's not hard to see, then, why the Brethren in Christ emphasize both *consecration* and *discipleship*: consecration is the inner act or attitude which results in a life of discipleship, a life patterned after the life and the teachings of Jesus. There is little question that a life so lived will be an outstanding one—that is, standing out as different in a sinful world. That shouldn't surprise us, however, when we recall what it means to be holy. It means we are "set apart" from the world.

No longer conformed

Most of us don't like to think of ourselves as "set apart" or "abnormal." We prefer to "fit in" and be "one of the gang." While that's OK in some cases, Christians also need to realize that we live in a world which often promotes anti-Christian values. The world has its ways and God has his, and though they're not *always* at odds with one another, the Scriptures have clear instructions for us when they are. These instructions are spelled out in the Apostle Paul's letter to the Romans: "Do not conform any longer to the pattern of this world, but be transformed by the renewing of your mind. Then you will be able to test and approve what God's will is—his good, pleasing and perfect will" (Romans 12:2)

From this and a host of other New Testament passages, the Brethren in Christ have concluded that Christians are called to *nonconformity*. This call has been interpreted and applied in various ways throughout our history, but it shouldn't be assumed that variety in application invalidates the call itself. Rather, it is the responsibility of each new generation of Christians to identify and then resist the anti-Christian values of its own particular culture. Resisting those values will mean defying cultural norms, and it's in that sense that we'll be abnormal, or "nonconformists."

Examples of nonconformity

The Brethren in Christ, over the course of our existence, have tried to interpret God's call to holiness and set ourselves apart according to God's standard. One way we have exhibited our nonconformity is by resisting *hedonism*, a view which maintains that pleasure is the chief aim in life. "How enjoyable will this be? How fun will this be?" Those are questions that many people—especially in Western society—ask as they make their day-to-day decisions. And while those questions are not wrong in and of themselves, the primary question for Christians must always be: "What is God's view of this?"

Evidence of hedonism is all around us, for example in the cheapening of the marriage bond. For some people, marriage has ceased to be "fun" anymore; it used to be pleasurable, but now the romance has worn off and it's just a lot of work. People who find themselves in this situation (and many Christians do find themselves here) have not necessarily sinned, but they are faced with a choice; and if their commitment to personal pleasure is greater than their commitment to God's view of marriage, the choice they make will likely be the wrong one.

Resisting *materialism* is a second way the Brethren in Christ have exhibited their nonconformity. Materialism is placing an undue or improper emphasis upon material things, from cash to cars to condominiums. While the folly of materialism is obvious (as Paul writes in 1 Timothy 6, "we brought nothing into the world, and we can take nothing out of it"), a lot of people live as though they actually *can* take it with them.

This being the case, there are a number of principles by which Christians ought to live, principles which contradict society's values. First of all, just because you want something and can afford it doesn't mean you ought to buy it. Second, things ought to be bought for their usefulness rather than for their status (in other words, "a Ford will get you there as effectively as a Mercedes"). Third, the notion that your kids deserve to "have it better" than you did should be questioned; in other words, love them by giving of yourself. And finally, *all* of your material wealth is God's; that is, he's just as concerned about the money you don't put in the offering plate as the money that you do.

A third way the Brethren in Christ have exhibited nonconformity over the years is by rejecting *militarism*. Militarism is a view which encourages people to put undue trust in weapons and armies, and may lead people to have unreasonable fear of citizens of other nations. It stands in contradiction to both the commands (Matthew 5:43-48) and the example (Matthew 26:52-54; Romans 5:8, 10) of Jesus. Therefore, the Brethren in Christ have renounced for themselves worldly ways of violence and self-preservation and have instead advocated peacemaking and sacrificial service.

Historically, this has worked itself out through something called "alternate service." During times of conscription, instead of becoming active parts of their country's military, many Brethren in Christ young men have chosen to register with the government as "conscientious objectors" (COs). In so doing, they indicated a willingness to serve society but, at the same time, refused their nation's call to arms.

Being open to instruction

Some people who are new to the Brethren in Christ find these ideas and forms of nonconformity difficult to understand because they are so different from our pre-Christian ways of thinking. Perhaps the idea of being different—separate—is troubling to you. If so, you needn't jump to the conclusion that you shouldn't join the Brethren in Christ Church. The Brethren in Christ Church doesn't demand that you be in agreement with its every doctrine in order to become a member. What the church asks (as stated in the Membership Covenant) is that you "consent to instruction in Bible doctrine" as presented in Brethren in Christ churches. We ask that you listen to and then prayerfully consider what the Brethren in Christ have historically said—and now say—about faithful living in a complex world. Only as we talk and listen to one another can we truly call ourselves "brothers and sisters in Christ," and can we arrive at what biblical nonconformity means for us today.

Conclusion

As we think about the many implications of nonconformity, it's plain to see that holiness entails a radical "setting apart" from the things of this world. At times, this can seem rather overwhelming, for the world exerts powerful influence. But in the face of that influence, we still have reason to rejoice, for we worship a holy God who is not only "set apart" himself, but who, in Christ, dealt with our sin and set us apart.

And the good news doesn't stop there, for the writer to the Hebrews states: "Both the one who makes men holy and those who are made holy are of the same family" (Hebrews 2:11). We are family, brothers and sisters *of* Christ, brothers and sisters *in* Christ.

Questions for reflection:

1. The commissioning of Isaiah in Isaiah 6 gives us a picture of God's holiness and our "potential" for holiness. What is Isaiah's initial reaction to the holiness of God (v. 5)? What provision does God make for Isaiah (v.7)? What is Isaiah's ensuing response (v.8)?

2. In what area of your life is it most difficult to pray "Thy will be done"? Read Christ's sermon in Matthew 5—7. Concentrate on Jesus' statements that start, "But I tell you. . . ." In what ways does Jesus tell us to do the will of God?

3. Have you ever found yourself in a situation where, as a Christian, you didn't fit in? How did it feel to be a "nonconformist"? Identify some concrete examples of contemporary nonconformity—being set apart for God.

4. What are some manifestations of hedonism in our society? Is it fair to say that hedonism and materialism are the two driving forces in contemporary Western society?

5. Evaluate the following statement: "For Christians, all people are either Christians or potential Christians; with such an understanding, there are no enemies—only people to love" (from "Study on Militarism," unpublished study document by the Brethren in Christ Board for Brotherhood Concerns, 1988).

Commitments to make

I, ______________________________, express desire and purpose to live a holy life, apart from sin and separated unto Christ.

I, ______________________________, consent to instruction in Bible doctrine.

---

[1]C. Frederick Buechner, "What Will You Be?" *The Princeton Seminary Bulletin*, Nov. 1984, p. 190.

[2]Luke Keefer, Jr., *Everything Necessary*, (Nappanee, IN: Evangel Press, 1984), p. 57.

4

Be Brothers and Sisters in Christ

"I covenant as a member of the Brethren in Christ Church to be loyal to this congregation . . . and to foster a spirit of Christian fellowship and oneness within the church."

Loyalty is a scarce commodity in our modern world. Husbands are disloyal to their wives (and vice versa); workers are disloyal to their employers; people are disloyal to their countries. The temptation to do what is convenient or personally advantageous is a strong one, one which seems to be getting stronger all the time. In the face of this trend, however, the Brethren in Christ membership covenant calls for loyalty. It calls for fellowship. It calls for unity.

The way it is versus the way it should be

Loyalty, fellowship, and unity certainly are out of step with the norm—even within the Christian Church. For the facts indicate that the typical "believer" isn't all that loyal to the group of people we call the church. A recent survey indicated that while 94 percent of the respondents believe in God and 80 percent believe that Jesus is the Son of God, only 40 percent attend church regularly.[1] Granted, regular church attendance is not one of the Ten Commandments, nor was it one of Christ's primary emphases, but it *is* indicative of one's commitment to a body of believers. Brethren in Christ people can't help but read the 40 percent figure above and think that something is drastically wrong.

That "something" might be summed up like this: a failure to grasp the dual nature of God's redemptive purposes. On the one hand, God wants to redeem *individuals*, persons who have made personal decisions to follow Jesus Christ. On the other hand, God desires a redeemed *people*—"a royal priesthood, a holy nation, a people belonging to God" who together declare his praises (1 Peter 2:9). Somehow, over the years, this latter half of God's desire has been increasingly disregarded by those who believe in Jesus.

But we are *Brethren* in Christ. Our denomination's name reflects our conviction that a "vertical" faith (a relationship with Jesus) is not enough; "horizontal" relationships with God's people are essential too. To call ourselves "Brethren in Christ" is to affirm our commitment to the two greatest commandments as identified by Jesus: (1) love the Lord your God with heart, soul, mind, and strength, and (2) love your neighbor as yourself (Mark 12:30-31). Moreover, to call ourselves "Brethren in Christ" is to capture the essence of how we would like to be in contrast to a world of isolation and loneliness: people committed to one another in the name of Jesus Christ.

The Church as "the family of God"

The horizontal *is* important. One clue to God's concern about the horizontal aspect of our faith is the myriad of pictures of the church drawn by New Testament writers. Paul Minear, in his book *Images of the Church in the New Testament*, identifies more than a hundred such pictures which, together, give us insight into the church and its mission.

It would be foolish to try to say which of these pictures is most meaningful or most significant. Individually, each has something unique to offer; together, they offer a more complete understanding of the church than any could offer on its own.

Images of the Church

The Salt of the Earth *(Matthew 5:13)*
The Light of the World *(Matthew 5:14)*
A City on a Hill *(Matthew 5:14)*
Branches of the Vine *(John 15)*
God's Building *(1 Corinthians 3:9)*
The Bride of Christ *(Ephesians 5:22-31)*
Strangers and Aliens in the World *(1 Peter 1:1; 2:11)*
The People of God *(1 Peter 2:9-10)*
A Holy Nation *(1 Peter 2:9)*
The Family of God *(1 Peter 4:17)*
The Body of Christ *(Romans 12:5)*
The Elect *(2 Timothy 2:10)*
A Chosen People *(1 Peter 2:9)*
A Royal Priesthood *(1 Peter 2:9)*
God's Household *(Ephesians 2:19)*
Fellow Citizens *(Ephesians 2:19)*
Children of Light *(Ephesians 5:8)*
God's Flock *(1 Peter 5:2-3)*
The Chosen Lady *(2 John 1:1)*
Abraham's Offspring *(Romans 4:16)*
Christ's Ambassadors *(2 Corinthians 5:18-21)*

These are taken primarily from Paul Minear's *Images of the Church in the New Testament*, Philadelphia, Westminster Press, 1960.

Nonetheless, there's one image which is particularly relevant to this chapter's emphasis on loyalty, fellowship and unity. It's an image drawn by the Apostle Paul when he refers to the Ephesians as "members of God's household" (Ephesians 2:19). The church is a family, *God's* family. He is our Father and we are his children, brothers and sisters in Christ.

Nearly everyone knows something about families, although for some persons, the mention of "family" brings painful memories. While there are many analogies we could draw between biological families and spiritual families, two will suffice here. First, being part of a family means having a place to belong, a place to feel at home. In other words, when families—biological *and* spiritual—function as they should, they provide a pocket of warmth in a cold world. This, however, does not negate a second point of analogy, and that is: life in the family isn't always a bed of roses. At home and at church, family life is a challenge—an adventure—which is frequently characterized by hard work.

In the paragraphs below, we will look at both sides of the coin, the challenges *and* the privileges.

The challenges of church membership

The Church of the Savior in Washington D.C. offers a booklet to persons exploring church membership which begins like this: "This is a dangerous book . . . for if one becomes committed to this way, all of life will be different. . . ." As far as I know, no Brethren in Christ congregation gives its prospective members a booklet like that, but, in reality, our view of membership is pretty much the same. We believe that your life will be (or is) markedly different because of your commitment to a local Brethren in Christ church.

Not that affirming the membership covenant does anything magical in and of itself; rather, the sincere commitment you make will work its way out in every aspect of life. It will affect the way you use your time. It will affect the way you use your talents. It will even affect the way you use your tongue—all for the sake of achieving three important goals: congregational loyalty, fellowship, and oneness.

Loyalty means that you will represent your congregation in a positive light, especially if those around you tend to be overly critical. You won't always agree with everything that happens in your local church or with everything your pastor does. But loyalty means you will look for the good in spite of occasional disappointment or frustration. It means you'll "stick with it" through thick and thin.

Fostering a spirit of fellowship means that, in spite of busy home and work schedules, you will take time to support, encourage and actively love your brothers and sisters in Christ. It doesn't mean you will attend every church-sponsored event or know every member intimately. But it does mean you'll "be there" for people who need you.

Finally, *fostering a spirit of oneness* means that you will love and listen, forgive and seek forgiveness. You may not see eye to eye with your brothers and sisters on every issue, but you will attempt to abolish walls between people rather than erect them.

Initially, these expectations are relatively foreign to us, neither valued nor pursued by the world in which we live. New Christians and old alike sometimes find them difficult to put into practice. Nonetheless, they represent the will of God, the Father of our family. And thus, with his help, we who are his children will seek to carry them out.

The privileges of church membership

There's no doubt about it: sometimes being a responsible church member is just plain hard. But, many times, it's just plain good. For in the church we'll find people who will share our joy and sorrow, people who will work, pray and play with us, and people who will help us grow in the faith and knowledge of Jesus Christ. Most of all, in the church we are privileged to not only give, but to receive three things for which human beings long: loyalty, fellowship and oneness.

Loyalty in the church means people are committed to give to you—just as you give to them—allegiance that transcends circumstances. We all face ups and downs in life, but ideally our pledge of loyalty means we'll stick together through thick and thin. It means that, as members of one another, we'll covenant to stand by one another in trying times.

Fellowship is the fruit of loyalty, a result of the trust it fosters. Although we sometimes speak of "fun and fellowship," fellowship is much more than having a good time together. It's a sense of belonging, of being a part of a group that cares. Fellowship means receiving strength and encouragement from supportive relationships.

A third privilege of membership is a sense of unity, or *oneness.* We're not all alike in the Brethren in Christ Church (praise the Lord for that!), but we do share this in common: our love for Jesus Christ. He makes us one; at the same time, he makes our differences tolerable, and even enjoyable. Being one in Jesus Christ gives us the freedom to revel in our God-given diversity.

Conclusion

One of the hymns in the Brethren in Christ hymnal begins, "The church of God is people," and indeed it is. And while we aren't perfect people, we are at least people who have made the same commitment: to love one another in the name of Jesus Christ. In one sense, that's a rather risky commitment to make, because God doesn't reveal in advance exactly what loving one another will entail. In another sense, however, it's not very risky at all, for the assurance of mutual care within the church is the best insurance policy on earth. Little wonder we Brethren in Christ love to sing:

> "Blest be the tie that binds our hearts in Christian love;
> The fellowship of kindred minds is like to that above."

Questions for reflection:

1. What kind of directives would Jesus give regarding church attendance? Would he require it? What would he require in regard to involvement in a local church? Why?

2. In what ways is a church like a family? In what ways is it different? Can you think of other scriptural analogies used to describe the church of Jesus Christ? (See 1 Peter 2:4-10; 1 Cor. 3:16 and 12:27.)

3. Dealing with conflict and hurt in constructive ways is essential to good family health. How do you do that in your biological family? How is that best done in the context of a church family? (See Matthew 18.)

4. How does (or would) a commitment to a local church change your life from day to day? How does (or would) it affect the way you use your time? your talents? your tongue?

5. One of the hymns in the Brethren in Christ hymnal describes the church as "diverse yet truly one" (from "We Are God's People," *Hymns for Praise and Worship*). In what ways do you see diversity in your church? In what way(s) are you "truly one"?

A commitment to make

I, ______________________________, covenant to be loyal to the ______________________________ congregation and to foster a spirit of Christian fellowship and oneness within the church.

---

[1] *The Gallup Report*, "Religion in America," April 1987.

5

Be Body Builders

"I covenant as a member of the Brethren in Christ Church to . . . support and sustain [this congregation's] services by my regular attendance and prayers, [and] contribute to the program of the church as the Lord prospers me."

In Chapter Two, we touched briefly on the idea that the Bible performs an equipping function, equipping its readers "for every good work" (2 Timothy 3:17). Good works might entail any number of things, but, for our purposes, we'll divide them into two categories: those done for the sake of our fellow believers and those done for the sake of non-believers. In this chapter, we will look at the former category; in Chapter Six, we will look at the latter.

Faith and works

The Brethren in Christ have long maintained the importance of good works in the lives of believers. In the words of Jesus: "A tree is recognized by its fruit" (Matthew 12:33). In other words, true faith in Jesus Christ will prove itself by bearing the fruit of good works.

This is not a "salvation by works" doctrine. The Apostle Paul is clear: salvation comes by faith in Jesus Christ and is *not* a result of the things we do (Romans 3:21-22, 27-28). We cannot save ourselves from sin and death. God alone can save.

Bearing this in mind, however, we must also hear James. According to James, a faith which is not accompanied by deeds is not a true faith, it is a dead one (James 2:14-26). Over the centuries, some Christians have had difficulty accepting the ideas of both Paul and James, but for the Brethren in Christ, this has never been a problem. Paul and James simply represent the two sides of the coin of faith: (1) we are saved by faith and (2) true faith manifests itself in good works. The ideas are complementary rather than contradictory.

It is significant that, in his discussion on faith and works, James utilizes two Old Testament figures: Abraham and Rahab. While Abraham and Rahab were very much alike in one sense—that is, in possessing a faith that led to action—they were hardly two peas in a pod. Abraham was a respected, Jewish male, the father of the Jewish nation; Rahab was a foreign woman of ill-repute, a prostitute. Which just goes to show: God uses *all kinds* of people when they're willing to put their faith in him.

The Church as the Body of Christ

The church is all kinds of people. In the previous chapter, we emphasized God's desire for unity in the church (John 17:23; Romans 15:5); but we do not want to interpret "unity" as everyone thinking alike, talking alike and acting alike. "Unity in diversity," *that's* the biblical understanding of the church, an understanding which is perhaps best portrayed by Paul's use of the "body" analogy in 1 Corinthians 12 and elsewhere.

The analogy is a good one. Just as physical bodies have many members (hands, feet, eyes, etc.), so has the body of Christ many members, each with his or her unique function. And just as no member of one's physical body is more important than the body itself, no member of one's church body is more important than the church itself. Nonetheless, each member *is* important; in fact, each member must do what he or she is supposed to do or the whole body suffers.

It is significant, then, that Paul precedes his "body talk" in 1 Corinthians 12 with a discussion of spiritual gifts. Spiritual gifts are special abilities given by God to believers for the purpose of strengthening the Church and spreading the gospel. These gifts do not appear in finished form, but are rather given in the form of seeds. Those who carefully nurture and use their spiritual gifts, yielding them back to God and his service, receive a generous return.

In the last number of decades, the Greek word for gifts, *charismata*, has been used to designate a particular movement within the Church, the "*charismatic* movement." It is also a correct use of the word to say that all churches are charismatic, for God bestows spiritual gifts upon all Christian believers, not just a select few or even those in a select few churches.

All believers, then, ought to ask themselves the question: "How can I do *my* part as a member of the body of Christ?" Paul's answer is rather clear: by using the spiritual gifts God has given you. In the midst of a chapter on church health, Paul writes: ". . . to each one of us grace has been given as Christ apportioned it" (Ephesians 4:7). That's not saving grace he's talking about, it's service grace—grace bestowed in the form of gifts and exhibited in "works of service, so that the body of Christ may be built up . . ." (v. 12).

"Building up the body"—as you can see, the analogy continues to hold. If you want a strong physical body, exercise. If you want a strong church body, exercise your gifts.

Service as a way of life

Exercising one's gifts through works of service is more than just a nice idea to the Brethren in Christ; it's absolutely central to who we are as a people. In fact, we're a little like the Quaker fellow who, during a silent Quaker meeting, was asked by a visitor: "When's the service going to begin?" His response was quick and to the point: "The service begins when the meeting is over." To him, spirituality was much more than a two-hour exercise on Sunday morning; it was a way of life. And though we might express ourselves a little differently than he did, the Brethren in Christ agree. We reject the notion of "Sunday morning Christianity."

Of course, Sunday morning is vitally important. Regular participation in community worship is an essential part of the Christian experience. Church attendance provides much-needed opportunities to adore God and be challenged by his Word. Worship inspires and energizes us for service. Sunday school and the worship hour also provide a consistent link with our brothers and sisters in Christ. They give us a forum to encourage one another, challenge one another, and remind one another why we're here.

And we are here to serve, as the Apostle Paul said in Ephesians 4:12. Your church, no matter how large or how small, is in great need of people who are willing to serve. Some of those needs are in structured ministries which continue from week-to-week and year-to-year (e.g. Sunday school teaching, janitorial or secretarial work, or singing in the choir). Other service opportunities are less formal, presenting themselves outside the bounds of any structured ministry (e.g. showing hospitality to or otherwise encouraging a brother or sister). Needless to say, the type of ministry you're involved in may vary, but the call to ministry does not. Each church member is called to be a minister, and your pastor or other congregational leaders would be glad to help you discover ways to be just that.

Giving as a way of life

Service is giving. It's giving of yourself, your time and your talents. But God calls his people to a second kind of giving. He calls us to give of our material possessions.

The Old and New Testaments both speak boldly about the

A Symbol of Service

In keeping with the commitment to serve, many Brethren in Christ congregations engage (once or twice a year) in the voluntary practice of footwashing. In Jesus' day, this lowly task was performed by slaves; it was therefore unexpected from one who was called "Master" and "Lord."

Jesus, however, was also called "Teacher" and, as a teacher, he knew the lesson of service was a hard one to learn. So he taught it the best way he knew how: by example. He washed his disciples' feet and then instructed them to "do as I have done for you" (John 13:15).

Some people argue that, in this modern age of paved roads and clean socks, the practice of footwashing is no longer relevant. On the practical level, that's true; the water in the basin rarely gets dirty. Moreover, there are many other ways to apply this principle of service more productively—providing babysitting to a young couple who need to have some time alone; doing volunteer work in a nursing home; helping repair the home of a widow; doing shopping for a shut-in.

On the symbolic level, however, the practice of footwashing and the lesson it provides is as relevant today as ever. When we allow our bodies to participate tangibly in worship in a ritual like this, we move our hearts to new levels of concentration on Christ and receptivity to God.

Footwashing continues to be a great "leveler" of persons, reminding its participants that all in Christ are one, and that all in Christ are called to serve.

importance of returning to God a portion of our material blessings. The basic principle in the Old Testament was "tithing," returning a tenth of one's earnings to God. While continuing to be a helpful standard, the New Testament replaced this principle with a new one: the principle of sacrificial giving (Luke 21:1-4; 2 Corinthians 8:1-15). "Giving sacrificially" is hard to define in theory, but, on the practical level, it means that many Christians will give more—possibly much more—than ten percent of their income to the Lord.

This ties in well with our covenant vow to "contribute . . . as the Lord prospers me." The church treasurer certainly appreciates large offerings. But giving to please people doesn't necessarily please God. God is pleased by giving that is done regularly, joyfully, and sacrificially. "Man measures by what is given. God measures by what is left."[1]

Christian stewardship calls not only for sacrificial giving, it calls for wise giving. In an era of "good causes" by the thousands, it's easy to be bad stewards with good intentions. Giving to your local church reduces that risk, for it provides the opportunity to give to a known entity. Together, church members decide the destination of their money. When it is dispersed, it is given to people who are accountable to them, and who therefore can be trusted. Giving to your local church is almost always a wise investment.

Conclusion

How does a person build up the body of Christ? The ways are many, but the essence is one: by being a giver. And from what we know about God, this should not surprise us. For God, by his very nature, is a giver. We see that in the *body* of Jesus Christ, to which God has given gifts of time, talents and money. More dramatically yet, we see that in the *person* of Jesus Christ, through whom God gave his life for a sinful world.

We are to be gracious and giving people, for our God is a gracious and giving God. "Thanks be to God for his indescribable gift!" (2 Corinthians 9:15).

Questions for reflection:

1. Is it possible to have true faith and not do good works? Is it possible to perform good works without having faith in Jesus Christ?

2. A variety of spiritual gifts are mentioned in Romans 12:6-8 and 1 Corinthians 12:4-11, 28. After examining these two passages, consider what your spiritual gifts might be. How might you use them in the context of your church?

3. Read John 13:1-17 and then consider the following questions:
   a. Why did Jesus perform an act that was reserved primarily for slaves?
   b. Why did Peter react as he did to Jesus' actions (v. 8)?
   c. Which do you find harder, serving others or letting others serve you?
   d. Does being a "towel-and-basin" Christian mean that we'll sometimes be taken advantage of?

4. React to the following statement from the 12th century abbot, Bernard of Clairvaux: "Learn the lesson that, if you are to do the work of a prophet, what you need is not a scepter but a hoe."

5. What does it mean to give sacrificially? What can we learn from the example of the Macedonian churches described in 2 Corinthians 8:1-5?

A commitment to make

I, ______________________________, covenant to support and sustain ______________________'s services by my regular attendance and prayers and contribute to her program as the Lord prospers me.

---

[1]John Zercher, "Let's Talk About Money" in *Lantern in the Dawn*, (Nappanee, IN: Evangel Press, 1980), p. 110.

6

Be Witnesses

"The purpose of the Brethren in Christ Church is to foster a fellowship of believers whose objective is to worship and obey the triune God, and to proclaim his gospel to all people."

Throughout the first five chapters of this book, we have examined membership vows as stated in the Brethren in Christ membership covenant. These vows lie in two specific areas: first, in the kind of people we ought to be (Chapters 1-3); and, second, in the kinds of things we ought to do to build a healthy Christian community (Chapters 4-5).

We now come to the third, and equally important, aspect of our life of faith, the one that looks outside the walls of the church to a world in need. Although no statements in the membership covenant deal directly with this aspect of the Christian life, the concepts of "church" and "mission" are, by their very nature, inseparable. The Brethren in Christ would undoubtedly agree with Emil Brunner's contention that "the church exists for mission as fire exists for burning." Therefore, the Brethren in Christ have included in the purpose statement of the church these words: "The purpose of the Brethren in Christ Church is to . . . proclaim [Christ's] gospel to all people."

The Church as a scattered community

It is tempting to think of the church only as gathered community. Of course, that's an important part of what we are, so important that the writer to the Hebrews advises his readers (including us): "Let us not give up meeting together, as some are in the habit of doing, but let us encourage one another . . ." (Hebrews 10:25). We gather together—we *need* to gather together—in order to give and receive encouragement.

Gathering, however, should not be seen as an end in itself but simply as a preface to scattering. Gathering readies us for mission; it *prepares* us for works of service beyond the comfortable confines of our Christian community. Indeed, this is the church's uniqueness: unlike so many organizations in our world, the church exists not for its own sake but for the sake of others. The church exists for a world in need.

This is why Jesus told his disciples: "You are the salt of the earth" (Matthew 5:13). Salt doesn't accomplish a whole lot on its own. It may look very attractive in a pretty, little saltshaker, but all in all, it just sits there. Once it gets out and goes to work, however, salt has a radically profound effect on nearly everything it touches. It flavors, it purifies, it preserves. In a sense, it *transforms* things that are otherwise flavorless, unclean and decaying.

"You are the salt of the earth," says Jesus. "You are my instruments for transforming a decaying world." It's a tremendous analogy; it's also a tremendous vote of confidence from the Son of God himself.

The salt of our lifestyle

There are a variety of ways God's scattered people can have a transforming effect in a decaying world. One way is by simply being Christian.

Donald Joy, a professor at Asbury Theological Seminary, teaches a course called "Discipleship Development through Trail Camping." The course is more than a notebook full of theory; it actually concludes with his students backpacking for a week with a small group of non-Christian teenagers.

Joy's guidelines for his students are simple: speak no religious words to the kids, don't use any strategies to convert them; just live with them and care for them. Joy's prediction for the week is straightforward: by the last night, virtually every kid will want to become a Christian. Joy's reasoning for his prediction is compelling: "Everyone wants to be wholly alive!"[1]

Joy's way of thinking is essentially no different from the Apostle Peter's. Peter, in the midst of a passage about repaying evil with good, writes: "Always be prepared to give an answer to everyone who asks you to give the reason for the hope that you have" (1 Peter 3:15). Peter's point is that when Christians act the way we ought to act, we're going to raise not only eyebrows, but questions in the minds of nonbelievers. These questions are what open the door for sharing about the hope that Jesus gives and the difference that he makes in our life.

The salt of verbal witness

Lives lived for God raise questions, but they don't answer them. Therefore, each and every Christian must be willing and ready to *verbally* give that "answer" Peter talks about.

Willingness is one side of verbal witness. Peter doesn't imply that the act of witnessing always comes naturally or easily. He doesn't even say there will always be a sense of eagerness. Willingness means that, despite our fears and uncertainties, we're going to be obedient to God. It means we're going to tell the story of God's love and recount its significance for our lives.

Telling our own story keeps our faith fresh and renewed. It should not surprise us that people who see our Christian behavior in the workplace or in recreational settings often are open to knowing us and the difference God has made in our lives. In many cases, God prepares those people in advance to hear what we have to say, and the experience is not scary at all, but full of satisfaction.

While willingness is the one side of verbal witnessing, *readiness* also is implied by Peter's phrase "always be prepared." Telling our own story is often a prelude to a gospel presentation or to answering questions that people might raise. Thus, regular and diligent Bible study will be beneficial. Although we needn't have large portions of Scripture memorized to be an effective Christian witness, we should know some, and a sustained immersion in the Scriptures will provide that "some." Regular Bible study provides a reservoir of knowledge which prepares us to answer reasonable questions in a wise and confident way.

The salt of social action

Social action—actively ministering to the physical and social needs of the world around us—is a third way for scattered Christians to be salt in a decaying world. This form of Christian witness flows out of the biblical view of persons, a view which asserts that people are more than just "souls to be saved." People are whole persons, and as such they have a variety of needs—spiritual, social and physical. It is therefore our responsibility as God's people to minister accordingly—spiritually, socially, and physically.

Of course, it would be impossible for every Christian to minister to every need in every situation he or she encounters. Furthermore, situations vary and thus demand different forms of Christian witness. Nonetheless, if you are faithfully salty, you'll doubtlessly have opportunities to minister in all three ways. With some people, you will share the gospel. With others, you will share a listening ear. With still others, you will share the gift of food and/or the gift of shelter. Sometimes one kind of opportunity will naturally lead to another.

The salt of world mission

Nearly three thousand years ago, the prophet Isaiah set for us a courageous example. The Lord needed someone to carry out his mission, and Isaiah's response was: "Here am I. Send me!" (Isaiah 6:8b). Over the centuries, Christians have followed Isaiah's example by expressing their willingness to do God's work *wherever* it might be. While for some that "wherever" has been just around the block, for others it's been way around the world.

The Brethren in Christ have long been a part of God's work among the nations. It's not that our North American ancestors didn't have anything to do at home; it's simply that they, like Isaiah, were compelled to "go and tell" (Isaiah 6:9). God called them, and so they went, sharing a gospel that transcended cultures, telling a story that transformed lives.

It's a process that continues today: God calling, people going. Of course, God doesn't ask every Christian to leave his or her culture in order to minister cross-culturally. It's possible, even probable, that God wants you right where you are. Nonetheless, it's unwise to assume that God will never ask you to "go." A faithful Christian is by necessity an open Christian, ready and willing to act upon God's surprising initiatives.

Conclusion

Indeed, our God is a God of surprises. The Scriptures bear witness to that fact, a fact which is perhaps most clearly demonstrated in the *people* God chooses to carry out his will:

Who else but God would have picked Moses to deliver the captives?

Who else but God would have picked Rahab to secure a new land?

Who else but God would have picked Peter to be one of the apostles of the Christian Church?

Surprising? Then again, who else but God would pick people like *us* to be his witnesses? But he has. And so we shall be.

Questions for reflection:

1. What does it mean to say that the church is both "a gathered and a scattered community"? How will that be evident in the life of the church?

2. Is it true that simply living a Christian life will have a transforming effect on the world around us? Is lifestyle evangelism a valid concept? Why or why not?

3. What factors make it hard to be a verbal witness? Is it likely that God regularly provides for us witnessing opportunities that we either miss altogether or choose to ignore?

4. What are some ways Christians are called to be involved in the social issues of our day? Is there a difference between social action and political action?

5. Have you ever considered missions work in another culture? What would it take to convince you that God was calling you into that kind of service?

A commitment to make

I, ______________________________, promise to be a witness for Jesus Christ in my God-given corner of the world, and to take an active interest in the church's mission to proclaim the gospel to all people.

---

[1]Donald M. Joy, *Walk On!* (Wheaton, IL: Scripture Press, 1988), pp. 11-12.

Appendix

A Brief History of the Brethren in Christ

One of the keys to understanding people is to know their background and how that background influences the way they look at themselves and their world. In order to make that determination quickly and accurately, counselors frequently use a tool called a genogram, a diagram of a person's family tree. Genograms often provide people with a fresh perspective on who they are.

Genograms are helpful because they reveal a very important fact of life: people are products of their past. That's true for individuals, and it's also true for groups of people like the Brethren in Christ. Being a product of our past doesn't mean we're enslaved to it. It simply means that our today is rooted in our yesterday, and that our present is influenced by our past. It means that we have been, and will continue to be, affected by the beliefs and practices of those who have gone before us.

Two essays by E. Morris Sider were a major resource for this section: "Our Historical and Theological Roots" and "A History of the Brethren in Christ," which appeared in *On Being Brethren in Christ,* published by Evangel Publishing House, Nappanee, IN.

Some of those beliefs and practices are discussed in the pages to follow, pages which represent a kind of genogram of the Brethren in Christ Church. After studying this genogram, you likely will understand from whence the Brethren in Christ Church

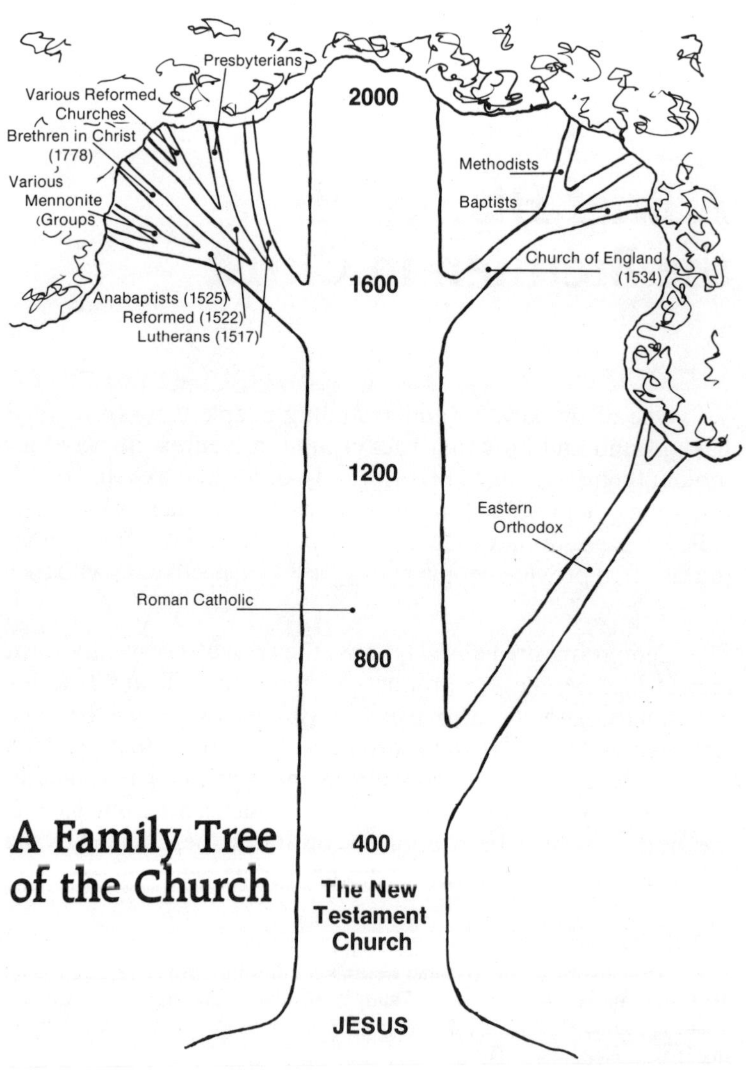

A Family Tree of the Church

has come. And if you do, you'll almost certainly be better equipped to serve its future.

The Protestant Reformation

For nearly 1500 years following Christ's death and resurrection, the Christian Church existed primarily as one institution: the Catholic Church. Not until Martin Luther and other reformers came along in the sixteenth century did events take place which ultimately led to an entirely new wing of the Church, the Protestant wing.

The Protestant reformers—for example, Martin Luther, John Calvin, Ulrich Zwingli—were far from uniform in their beliefs. They were, however, united in certain fundamental beliefs, some of which set them in direct opposition to the doctrines and practices of the Roman Catholic Church. "The just shall live by faith" was one such fundamental, a belief which stood in opposition to a growing salvation-by-works emphasis in the Catholic Church. A second basic belief held by the Reformers was that the Bible—not the Roman Catholic hierarchy—was the ultimate authority in matters of faith and practice. A third belief that set the Protestants apart from the Catholic Church was a commitment to "the priesthood of all believers." The Reformers believed that every person had direct access to God. They thus denied the need for ordained priests to serve as intermediaries.

While these three Protestant reforms might seem rather modest to 20th century Christians, they were no doubt radical ones in their day. Many people were persecuted for advocating those ideas, and some were even killed. Still, there was a group of courageous believers who felt that these basic reforms, while good, didn't go far enough. This group promoted ideas that were even more radical. This group was called the Anabaptists.

Our Anabaptist roots

The literal meaning of the term Anabaptist is "re-baptizer," *ana* being a Greek prefix meaning "again." To the Anabaptists, baptism was the public sign that a conversion experience had already taken place. Since infants couldn't have a conversion experience, the Anabaptists rejected the traditional Christian practice of infant baptism and promoted instead a radically new practice: believers' (or adult) baptism. For the first generation Anabaptists, this meant being rebaptized, since as Roman Catholics they had already been baptized a first time as infants. This practice scandalized other Christians of their day who disparagingly—and fittingly—dubbed these rebaptizers "Anabaptists."

The Anabaptists held other beliefs which their contemporaries found scandalous. For example, the Anabaptists believed that only those who had been converted and baptized comprised the body of Christ; to them, the church by definition consisted of committed believers only. This idea—an emphasis on the "visible church"—stood in direct opposition to the prevailing view that the church consisted of everyone who had ever been baptized, regardless of their present commitment. The Anabaptists were unique in this way. They held a high view of the church and exhibited a strong desire to maintain its purity. The practice of disciplining members (according to Matthew 18) was not uncommon.

The Anabaptists' high view of the church contrasted sharply with their low view of the world, a combination which gave birth to another radical concept: the separation of church and state. While other 16th century reformers retained the Roman Catholic position which advocated a close relationship between church and state, the Anabaptists argued that Christians could either serve the kingdom of God or the kingdom of the world, but not both. They believed that Christ's followers were to be separate from the world—in the world, but not of the world (John 17:15-16).

One thing this meant in practice was a refusal to serve in the military. The Anabaptists knew of Jesus' command to love one's enemies and, to them, that command took priority over national interests, including national security. Nonresistance was but one of many examples of the Anabaptists' commitment to discipleship, a commitment which meant walking according to the example and the commands of Jesus in every area of life.

As you might suspect, the beliefs of the Anabaptists weren't exactly music to the authorities' ears. Persecution of the Anabaptists abounded in the 16th and 17th centuries, much of which is well-documented. Sources such as *The Martyrs' Mirror* speak of beheadings, drownings, and burnings at the stake. Consequently, many Anabaptists spent their lives on the run, looking for places where they could practice their faith in peace. Some eventually fled to the New World, the soon-to-be United States of America. Here they found respite, among other places, in the land of William Penn, the land we now call "Pennsylvania."

Our Pietist roots

Many of the Anabaptists who settled in Pennsylvania had been influenced, in one way or another, by a Dutch Anabaptist leader named Menno Simons. The "Mennonites," as they were called, settled largely in Pennsylvania's Lancaster County near the Susquehanna River, and it is primarily from these people that the Brethren in Christ emerged in the late 1770s.

"Emerge" is a much better description of what happened than the term "split." It seems that, over time, a number of these Lancaster County Mennonites were exposed to and affected by a pervasive religious influence known as "Pietism," an influence which gradually pulled them away from the Mennonite mainstream. Pietism, which began in Germany around 1675, emphasized a warm, personally-experienced religion in a day when religion had turned cold and rational. It put the heart back into religion, replacing dogma with devotion. Not surprisingly, the movement spread rapidly throughout a spiritually hungry Europe and eventually came to America via the Moravians and the Dunkards. These two groups settled, among other places, in central Pennsylvania.

The warm-heartedness of Pietism spawned great revivals throughout 18th century America, including Lancaster County.

Some of the Mennonites who were touched by these revivals began to meet together in small groups to discuss their experiences, study the Scriptures and pray. As they did so, they felt increasingly dissatisfied with their traditional Anabaptist groups, groups which were generally devoid of the pietistic emphasis on a warm-hearted conversion experience. They were not eager, however, to abandon their Anabaptist emphases—emphases that, for the most part, other pietistic groups lacked. They faced a dilemma that was ultimately solved in the formation of a new church: the Brethren in Christ.

The early Brethren in Christ didn't call themselves "Brethren in Christ," they called themselves "the Brethren." It wasn't long, however, until they became known as the "River Brethren" because of their proximity to the Susquehanna River. That designation stuck for nearly a hundred years, until the outbreak of the Civil War. It was at that time that the River Brethren changed their name to "Brethren in Christ." (The reason for the name change remains a mystery even to this day.) The Canadian Brethren, on the other hand, didn't adopt the name "Brethren in Christ" until much later, 1933 to be exact. For years prior to that, they were known as "Tunkers," a designation which likely was rooted in their (and our) preferred mode of baptism, trine immersion (from a kneeling position in the water, immersed three times forward).

Our first century (1780-1880)

For nearly a hundred years, the early Brethren retained much of their original character, clearly combining the Anabaptist and pietistic elements of their faith. As pietists, they stressed the centrality of a heartfelt conversion experience; as Anabaptists, they stressed separation from the world and a radical obedience to the ways of Jesus (discipleship).

These theological emphases had practical implications. Involvement in "worldly" activities, such as politics and certain kinds of amusement (e.g. card playing) were forbidden. Clothing was simple (or "plain"), unadorned by jewelry, bright colors and frills. The women wore bonnets; the men, broadbrimmed black hats. This plain dress made the Brethren in Christ quite noticeable in their communities, a fact that, for the most part, didn't bother them. In fact, it corresponded nicely with their belief that the people of God should stand out as different in a sinful world.

The early Brethren were indeed aliens in the world, but they were at home with one another. They relied heavily on one another for counsel and encouragement. They met together regularly (in homes, not church buildings) and encouraged one another through preaching and the sharing of testimonies. They shared their money, their food, their homes, and took special measures to care for those in physical or financial need. They likewise cared for one another's spiritual needs, calling one another to accountability, confessing sins to one another and prayerfully advising one another on major decisions.

They knew they were not alone in the world, for they were truly *Brethren* in Christ.

Our first period of transition (1880-1910)

In his history of the Brethren in Christ, *Quest for Piety and Obedience*, the late Carlton O. Wittlinger characterizes the years 1880-1910 as the "first period of transition." It was during this thirty-year period that six major changes (and many minor ones) occurred in the life of the Brethren in Christ, changes that significantly modified the way we look at ourselves and our world.

Two of the six changes fall in the category of evangelism. Even though the Brethren in Christ believed in evangelism earlier, it wasn't until this period of transition that the church began to do it in systematic ways.

One of these systematic ways was *cross-cultural missions*. In 1894, the Brethren in Christ began a mission work in the city of Chicago and, in 1898, began their first foreign mission work in the African nation of Rhodesia (now Zimbabwe). Soon our foreign mission work spread to Zambia and then to India. Today, the Brethren in Christ Board for World Missions sponsors works in more than fifteen different countries. The faithfulness and hard work of our missionaries is apparent in the fact that there are currently more Brethren in Christ members abroad than there are in Canada and the United States combined.

The second systematic evangelism technique adopted during this period was the *protracted meeting*, or what is commonly referred to nowadays as "revival meetings." Protracted meetings were a series of services in churches and/or tents designed to convert the soul of the unconverted and renew the fervor of the converted. Although they have been modified to a degree (some are called spiritual life, or renewal meetings, and last for fewer days), revival meetings continue to play an important role in the lives of many congregations.

A third major change during the years 1880-1910 was the incorporation of a practice used in many Protestant churches—*Sunday school.* Surprising as it may be, the idea of Sunday school was a controversial one in Brethren in Christ circles, and it generated much heated debate at Brethren in Christ conferences. The pro-Sunday school faction, however, eventually won the day and many congregations began programs emphasizing both evangelism and the spiritual nurture of children and youth.

A fourth major change, also educationally-related, was the founding of *educational institutions*. The early Brethren in Christ were not formally educated and were somewhat skeptical of its value for Christians. This viewpoint changed, however, as they became increasingly aware that education would help advance the gospel. The result was the creation of the Messiah Bible School and Missionary Training Home, founded in Harrisburg, Pennsylvania in 1909 and moved to Grantham in 1911. Other educational endeavors soon followed—Beulah College in Upland, California; Jabbok Bible School in Thomas, Oklahoma; and Ontario Bible School near Fort Erie, Ontario. The Pennsylvania and Ontario schools continue today as Messiah College and Niagara Christian College, respectively.

The fifth major change during this thirty year period was the development of a denominational periodical, the *Evangelical Visitor*. This periodical, which has now been published for over a hundred years, was founded with the following objectives in mind: "Devoted to the Spread of Evangelical Truths and the Unity of the Church" (*Evangelical Visitor*, August 1, 1887). It served those functions well then, and continues to do so today.

Last, but far from least, is the sixth major change during the years 1880-1910: the inclusion of *Wesleyan holiness* as a third major theological stream to go along with our Anabaptist and pietistic roots. Wesleyan holiness derives its name from John Wesley, the founder of the Methodist movement, whose teachings on sanctification were widely influential.

Wesley maintained that although Christians may be converted, they still have a carnal nature which gives them trouble. The Holy Spirit, however, is able to deal with this carnal nature. As Christians offer (consecrate) themselves fully to God, the Holy Spirit fills their lives, giving them power over sin and freeing them from the bondage of carnality. Wesley called this power and freedom the "sanctified life" or "Christian perfection."

The emphasis on the sanctified life came to the Brethren in Christ through contacts with other groups who held this doctrine. Certain segments of the denomination accepted Wesleyan holiness readily and promoted it boldly. Others, however, were reluctant to accept it, preferring the Brethren's original view of sanctification as a growth process from conversion to death without a "second definite work of grace." After much debate, the church officially adopted and many people accepted the Wesleyan view that holiness comes through an act of grace (sanctification) that cleanses the heart of its inclination to sin.

Today, this doctrine continues to be promoted effectively by the holiness camp meetings, the first of which was founded in 1936 in Roxbury, Pennsylvania. Other Brethren in Christ camp meetings are located in Ohio (Memorial Holiness Camp), Ontario (Niagara Camp) and Florida (Camp Freedom).

Our second period of transition (1945-1975)

In the thirty or so years following World War II, the Brethren in Christ went through another period of fast-paced and far-reaching changes. Part of the reason for these changes was sociological in nature. As much as the Brethren wanted to "be in but not of the world," societal changes following World War II affected them keenly. For example, with the demand for farmers decreasing, and with opportunities in other areas such as business and the professions attracting them, many Brethren in Christ people moved from farms into towns and cities, places where they were confronted by new people and new ideas. These factors in turn forced the Brethren in Christ to evaluate how they could best relate and witness to people—Christians and non-Christians—in a modern world.

The adjustments were many and varied. Over the course of a few decades, most Brethren in Christ people abandoned the strict practices of plain dress (although not the principle of modesty). Pastors, who had previously made their living in secular jobs, were now hired by their congregations so they could devote their full energies to the work of the church. Church architecture became less austere, and musical instruments, once considered worldly, were now accepted in homes and even in worship services. Activities such as athletic competitions, summer camps and Bible quizzing were added to make church life more attractive to young people.

In sum, the second period of transition moved the Brethren in Christ Church away from its sectarian past and toward what might be called the mainstream of North American evangelicalism. The Church's decision during this time to join ecumenical groups such as the National Association of Evangelicals (NAE), the Christian Holiness Association (CHA) and, in Canada, the Canadian Holiness Federation (CHF) and Evangelical Fellowship of Canada (EFC) contributed to that trend. While we've undoubtedly been influenced—theologically and practically—by affiliating with other Christians, it's neither accurate nor fair to say the Brethren in Christ are "just another evangelical denomination." We continue to be unique: pietistic Anabaptists who stress the importance of discipleship and holy living.

Conclusion

It's been over two hundred years since the Brethren first gathered near the Susquehanna River to talk and to pray. As the years have gone by, the changes have been many, but the guiding principles of the Brethren in Christ have remained the same. We continue to stress the importance of living in right relationship with God and other people. We continue to stress the importance of the Bible's authority over our lives. We continue to stress the importance of new birth, an experience that only begins a journey of obedient discipleship and holy living.

The journey is a challenging one, but the fact that we take the journey together makes it a good one.

You're invited to come along.

Questions for reflection:

1. The three theological streams of the Brethren in Christ are Anabaptism, Pietism and Wesleyanism. What are the emphases of these three streams? How do you see them being emphasized in your local church? Is your congregation influenced by any other type of theological influence?

2. Do you think the founders of the Brethren in Christ were wise to begin a new group rather than working within already existing denominations? Would you encourage members today to split from our church if they disagreed on some parts of our denomination's teachings?

3. Do you consider "Brethren in Christ" to be a good name for a denomination? If you were able to choose a different name to represent who we are, what would you choose?

4. Do we, as a denomination, continue to have a high view of the church and a low view of the world? What evidence can you give to support your answer?

5. Is the concept of mutual care and brotherhood an outmoded one? How can we continue to foster community in such an individualistic world?

6. It is often said that the six changes that took place during our first period of transition (1880-1910) altered the way we related to the world. Why do you think that was the case?

7. Was the move away from our "sectarian past" a choice we made or was it inevitable? What are the advantages and disadvantages of being more closely aligned with mainstream evangelicalism and society as a whole?

THE STORY OF DIRK WILLEMS

In the year 1569, a pious and faithful brother by the name of Dirk Willems was apprehended at Asperen, Holland, and charged with the crime of being rebaptized as an adult. Concerning his apprehension, it is stated by trustworthy persons that when he fled, he was hotly pursued by a thief-catcher. There had been cold weather the night before and Dirk took a shortcut over a frozen pond. However, when the thief-catcher tried to follow him, the ice gave way and the thief-catcher broke through. Dirk perceived that his would-be captor was in danger of his life, so he quickly returned and helped him out of the water, thus saving his life.

Understandably, the thief-catcher wanted to let him go, but the town marshall reminded him of his oath and demanded that he take Dirk into custody. And the thief-catcher did so. Dirk was seized, imprisoned, and made to stand trial. He was found "guilty" and was later put to death at a lingering fire. Yet through it all, Dirk endured with great steadfastness, confirming the genuine faith of the truth with his death and blood as an example for all Christians.

—from J. van Braght's *Martyrs Mirror* (1660)

(For classroom use in Session 3)

Discipleship Means "Jesus is Lord

(Luke 14:25-35)

VERSES	MEANING
1. Hate your ____________________. (vv. 25-26)	1.
2. Carry your ____________________. (v. 27)	2.
3. Count the ____________ of following Jesus, for it means giving up ________ ____________________. (vv. 28-33)	3.
4. Unsalty salt is ____________________. (v. 34)	4.

He who has ears to hea

APPLICATION

Think about *your* life. What is most important to you?

How might this most important thing conflict with Christ's claim that he is Lord?

t him hear! (v. 35)

(For classroom use in Session 4)

ARTICLE XXXI
MEMBERSHIP REQUIREMENTS (A)

A. Persons considered for membership shall testify to a personal experience of God's saving grace in their heart and to confession of faith in Jesus Christ as their Savior and Lord, and shall give evidence of the new life in Christ.

B. They shall be open to the teaching of the Scripture, to the leadership of the Holy Spirit, and to the counsel of the church in questions of life and practice.

C. Applicants shall be baptized by trine immersion as a witness of faith and discipleship. Rebaptism is not required for those who have been baptized by another mode of believers' baptism subsequent to their rebirth.

D. Applicants shall express a desire to enter into a relationship of Christian love, fellowship and brotherhood with the members of the congregation and to cooperate with the polity of the Brethren in Christ Church.

E. Applicants shall affirm their acceptance of the above through the following membership covenant.

Membership Covenant

As a member of the Brethren in Christ Church, I accept the Bible as the Word of God in which is revealed the way of salvation and the guide for faith and conduct. I witness to a personal experience of God's saving grace in my heart, and express desire and purpose to live a holy life, apart from sin and separated unto Christ. I covenant as a member of the Brethren in Christ Church to be loyal to this congregation, to consent to instruction in Bible doctrine, to support and sustain the services of the congregation by my regular attendance and prayers, to contribute to the program of the church as the Lord prospers me, and to foster a spirit of Christian fellowship and oneness within the church.

Taken from the 1988 edition of the *Manual of Doctrine and Government*, p. 71.

Prayer Journal

These pages are provided for you to list your prayer requests and the answers. Also list praises.

Date *Prayers and praises* *Date and Answer*

Date	*Prayers and praises*	*Date and Answer*

Date	Prayers and praises	Date and Answer